4393:

From a Ride to His Will

-

By Leroy "Plump" Rogers

DEDICATION

To my beloved Grandmother, although you've gained your heavenly wings, I know you are still watching over me. I want you to know how much I miss you and honor you as the woman of faith that you were.

I dedicate this book to you to simply show you how much has changed in my life. Many of the lessons of life you taught me, I apply to my life daily. It's my prayer that you are proud even from Heaven. Love you Ma.

TABLE OF CONTENTS

FOREWORD

Isaiah 40:31, NKJV, reminds us, *"But those who wait on the Lord shall renew their strength. They shall mount up with wings like eagles. They shall run and not be weary. They shall walk and not faint."*

This passage of scripture is a glimpse of *"4393: From a Ride to His Will"*; I consider it an honor to pen a portion of this literary work by Leroy "Plump" Rogers. Leroy shares how his incarceration period has developed his relationship with God and how he learned how to forgive others.

Just as the aforementioned scripture stated, "Those who wait"; Leroy has been incarcerated for 30 years. He understands that God is not bound by time but divinely He will come and rescue His children in due time. *"4393: From a Ride to His Will"*, will assist and encourage the reader on how patience plays an important role in our relationship with our Heavenly Father.

There are thousands of wrongfully convicted persons throughout the United States. This is a sector of our criminal justice system that is very dear to me and has taken a greater part of my non-profit organization, Living My Purpose Fully, Inc.™

*"**4393: From a Ride to His Will**",* offers not only how to develop patience but a relationship with God, self-development, and

development of the new narrative from an old adage, "All inmates are the same." Because of my faith, I know this to be not true. We are all uniquely and wonderfully made, flawed, and not perfect.

It's my prayer you are encouraged and inspired as Leroy "Plump" Rogers shares his story. I am so proud of his accomplishment and how God will get the glory in this story and how many lives will be saved.

Cassandra L. Clark
Executive Director
Living My Purpose Fully, Inc.

INTRODUCTION

April 3, 1993, changed the life of many. The State of Florida had a flux of tourist robberies, and several were killed. The most publicized case is that of the German tourist, horrifically killed in Miami. This case changed laws and rental car companies' regulations. Many were arrested and convicted to life sentences.

"*4393: From a Ride to His Will*", told by Leroy "Plump" Rogers, which was a co-defendant of the German tourist murder and robbery case; shares how his life changed in a matter of minutes. A young father catching a ride in the back seat, to go see his newborn daughter.

Leroy wasn't the driver of the vehicle that allegedly killed the German tourist, nor did he rob anyone. Due to the high publicity of this murder, the local, and state governments, and German Consulate demanded a suspect immediately. The case was investigated unfairly, no DNA was collected from Leroy, evidence was planted, testimonies were coerced, the eyewitness testimony was coached, and the trial was a 'rat race'. Although the life of the German tourist was lost, it was not under any criminal activity or cause of Leroy Rogers.

In *"4393: From a Ride to His Will"*, Leroy shares the different emotions he felt over the past 30 years. He expressed feelings of abandonment, and low self-esteem as a child, and is now an incarcerated father of two (2) small children. This story is very similar to the biblical story of Joseph. Joseph was thrown in jail after being wrongfully accused.

Although both men were wrongfully accused, God was with them and showed them favor. God isn't a perspective of persons, what He will do for one, He will do for another. Leroy believes by faith that the day is drawing near when his name will be called to come home.

CHAPTER 1

"I Call Upon You Lord"
Jeremiah 33:3

Peter was a man of great faith and bold action. But his brash style sometimes led him to make humiliating mistakes more than a faithful disciple. I'm reminded of Luke 22:54-62, regarding Peter denying Christ to the servant girl that had identified him.

I can relate when it comes to falling short of our own expectations. Learning to obey God is a process and failures are a part of our development as humble servants. The Lord doesn't reward rebellion or wrongdoing but blesses those who repent and embrace chastisement for growth. So be pliable in the Lord's hands. I thank him for using my failures to benefit others while bringing Him glory.

Walking with God in dark times may continue until God's purpose is accomplished. The Lord's plan was to prepare Joseph to rescue his family as well as the nation of Egypt from famine, but first God placed

Joseph in the role of a servant, where he earned favor with the Egyptian leaders. He was then sent to prison where the Lord extended him kindness and favor (Genesis 39:21, NKJV) positioning him to interpret Pharaoh's dream. Through these difficult situations, Joseph was chosen by Pharaoh to lead Egypt and save the nation from famine as God planned.

We learn in both the dark and light. Besides discovering God's faithfulness Joseph learned to handle high and low positions to say no to temptation and to discern God's presence. What we learn in the darkness we are to share in the light.

Joseph did not let imprisonment discourage him from helping others, in fact when interpreting Pharaoh's dreams; he openly shared his faith and God-given knowledge. (Genesis 41:15-16, NKJV)

No one goes looking for hard times, but they seem to find some. Some of us regularly, instead of fearing them we can trust God and embrace His plan knowing He uses them for his glory and gain.

In Ecclesiastes 3:1, God reveals many things, first He reminds me that his timing is not my own. He says that *"to everything, there is a season, a time for every purpose under heaven."* God knows the right time for everything in my life to bloom. Second, I understood better that God's version of patience is not mine.

CHAPTER 2

God's Purpose, My Transformation

As a young man growing up, I was very stellar in things I wanted to do when I became an adult. I loved helping the elderly when I attended Sunday School, and sports was my second nature.

Then there was my purpose, no matter what I did I prayed. I was so grateful to have my grandmother, Elizabeth Green. She taught me the word of God. I lost her in April 2006, I lost my everything to the horrible disease of Alzheimer's. It seemed as if my whole life changed. I felt deflated and defeated. I began to process her goodness and how much she loved the Lord; and all that she instilled in me. I knew I had to be strong.

My transformation was very simple; all I really have now is God. After being incarcerated since the age of 23 and now being 53 years old.

Being in a system, where if you lose focus, you lose your sanity, and your desire to achieve your goals. You have all sorts of people from all walks of life. You have those that are manipulative and difficult people. As for me, I was blessed to get a dose of encouraging words. I had to pray without ceasing, never quench the Holy Spirit but commit to living a holy life. "Be strong in Christ Jesus and in the power of His Might." (Ephesians 6:10)

Life seems so unjust, so unfair the pain of rejection is almost more than I can bear. So, I had to learn how to let go of resentment and bitterness. I prayed *"Father, help me to let go of all bitterness and resentment. You are the One who binds up and heals the brokenhearted. I receive your anointing that breaks and destroys every yoke of bondage. I receive emotional healing by faith in your Word."* Isaiah 53:5, says *"But He was wounded for our transgressions, He was bruised for our iniquities; the chastisement for our peace was upon Him, and by His stripes, we are healed." "Thank you for giving me the grace to stand firm until this process is complete."*

Amen

CHAPTER 3

God's Promise to Bless Me

I had to stand on the promises of God and reflect on them daily. I leaned into these scriptures as my daily bread.

Luke 6:38, NKJV
"Give, and it will be given to you: good measure, pressed down, shaken together, and

running over will be put into my bosom. For with the same measure that you use, it will be measured back to you."

II Corinthians 9:8, NKJV

"And God is able to make all grace abound toward you, that you, always having all sufficiency in all things, may have an abundance for every good work."

Deuteronomy 28:2-3,6,8,12 NKJV

"Blessed shall you be in the city and blessed shall you be in the country. Blessed shall you be when you come in and blessed shall you be when you go out. And all these blessings shall

come upon you and overtake you. You, because you obey the voice of the Lord your God."
"The Lord will command the blessing on you in your storehouses and in all to which you set your hand, and He will bless you in the land which the LORD your God is giving you. The Lord will open to you His good treasure, the heavens, to give the rain to your land in its season, and to bless all the work of your hand."

Psalms 35:27, NKJV

"Let them shout for joy and be glad, who favor my righteous cause; and let them say continually, "Let the LORD be

magnified, who has pleasure in the prosperity of His servant."
II Peter 1:3, NKJV
"As his divine power has given to us all things that pertain to life and godliness, through the knowledge of Him who called us by glory and virtue."

Numbers 13:30, NKJV
"Then Caleb quieted the people before Moses, and said, "Let us go up at once and take possession, for we are well able to overcome it."

Psalms 37:4, NKJV
"Delight yourself also in the Lord, and He shall give you the desires of your heart."

Malachi 3:11a, NKJV
"And I will rebuke the devourer for your sakes."

Isaiah 54:17a, NKJV
"No weapon formed against you shall prosper."

By my faith in the Lord Jesus Christ, I declare that all obstacles and hindrances to my prosperity are now dissolved.

Psalms 23:1, NKJV
"The LORD is my shepherd; I shall not want."

John 10:10b, NKJV

"I have come that they may have life and that they may have it more abundantly."
Psalms 1:3, NKJV
"He shall be like a tree planted by the rivers of water, that brings forth its fruit in its season, whose leaf also shall not wither; and whatever he does shall prosper." If it is done in accordance with God's will for your life.

Proverbs 10:22, NKJV
"The blessing of the Lord makes one rich, and He adds no sorrow with it."

I am blessed in my finances, my relationships, and my health. They all flourish in the Lord. His blessings overtake me in all areas of my life, and I receive them. I would take these scriptures and personalize them, as I was speaking with God. I was always taught to repeat the Word back to God in our prayers. This was my first fruit of each day God gave me breath.

CHAPTER 4

The Greatness of God

My Prayer:

Lord extend yourself through me in all areas of my life fully and completely, that I may give you glory, honor and praise unto you. I decree and declare you to be on the throne of my life in and over all areas of my life. Lord Jesus Christ, you are the author and the finisher of my faith. To God be the glory."

Prayer is like therapy for me. I know that even if God doesn't answer right away, He's working. He speaks to my heart through His Word, songs, and even other people.

I asked God, *"What do you want from my life?"* In my clearest consciousness, I heard God's reply.

God's Plan:

He said to me, *"Everything you have been through I have saved you for a purpose and now I am incubating you for a season. I'm reinventing you, making you like a diamond. When you get out, you will be a light and an example to others, you will spread the good news that the same way I saved you I will save them."*

Going on in with God, my grandmother taught me to put my trust in Jesus Christ for salvation when I was a child and trust His love for me when life seems uncertain. I felt like everything in life was rigged and the cards were stacked against me. God used every trial to increase my strength and confidence.

CHAPTER 5

Pressing Through Trials, Only God

I was convinced that I was unworthy, unloved, and unimportant; that's how I felt growing up and Satan worked hard to cement those lies into my belief system. Then I realized if *"God with me who* can be against me." (Romans 8:31, NKJV)

Then I heard the Holy Spirit say, *"You need to do what God is calling you to do. You will be ok. He will be with you."* God showed up and showed out. God promises that I'm never alone, He is with me and within me. God is faithful, and love and His timing are perfect.

When you change, your mindset changes for the better; when you seek God your life will change forever.

My alter ego has led me to some very dark places with the concept that "I'm a man before anything" and disregarding that it was only God who has kept me. I only can hear his voice reminding me that HE is I AM. John 8:58 says, *"Jesus said to them, most assuredly, I say to you before Abraham was, I AM."*

Not only did He remind me that He is *I AM* but in Psalms 111:9c, he continues to remind me of his marvelous names, *"Holy and Awesome is HIS name."* As I received emotional healing by faith according to your Word in Isaiah 53:5d, *"And by His stripes, we are healed."*

I thank you for giving me the grace to stand firm until this process is complete.

CHAPTER 6

My Turning Point

Everyone faces challenges whether it's financial difficulties, a health crisis, or personal trauma, we all struggle through hardships at some point.

Our first instinct is to pray and how we do so is very important. Just as David praises

God for his protection even as he begs for refuge. I truly acknowledge God's ability to handle anything and everything that comes my way. Another way to face challenges through prayer is by inviting others to join in this requires courage, especially for special people.

During my incarceration, God has blessed me to have someone in my life that is very, very special to me. Her name is Cassandra Clark, and we've known each other for the past 25 years of our lives. This spiritually anointed one has been given a gift to help save people through her prayers and intercession.

She is talented, a goddess, a queen, an international bestselling author, and has achieved some great accolades, a religious commentary writer, a visionary but most of all a mother, grandmother, and loving sister and she loves the Lord.

Ms. Cassandra is brilliant, the true example of a humble woman of Christ. In the process of her patience, Cassandra's time and effort have paid off, she thrives in her ministry; she loves the people of God. *"Love prospers when a fault is forgiven." (Proverbs 17:9,* NLT)

Gravitating to her aura is everything, she is blessed with her traits and qualities. As an accomplished author, she shares some unique stories about God our Savior and how her transformation was her calling. She is present and willing to serve, teach and preach the Gospel. I've been interceding in prayer for this amazing sister.

CHAPTER 7

Faith Makes the Man

I was always curious about how I can learn from Jesus' example of manhood and spiritually nurture my family with Christ-like love. Present and willing to serve when I'm tired and in need of refreshment I remember the Lord's promise, *"For My Yoke is*

easy and My burden is light."
Matthew 11:30, NKJV

My assignment was to ask God to release my anointing and renew my mind so that my heart can receive this great restoration.

"Awesome Faith"

Thirty (30) years of God's faithfulness gave me so much passion for Him and compassion for people.

"A Heart for God"

"The Lord describes David as a "man after His heart."
1 Samuel 13:14, NKJV

"The Lord is sovereign over all things; He is our Father. He

promises to "never leave us nor forsake us."
Deuteronomy 31:8b, NKJV

"Fear not, for I am with you; be not dismayed, for I am your God."
Isaiah 41:10a, NKJV

"Oh, give thanks to the LORD! Call upon His name; make known His deeds among the peoples! Sing to Him, sing psalms to Him; talk of all His wondrous works! Glory in His holy name; Let the hearts of those rejoice who seek the LORD! Seek the Lord and His strength Seek His face evermore!"
Psalms 105:1-4, NKJV

I dedicate this book to all of those who struggle in the war against worry. May each of us find peace by resting and rejoicing in the promises of God.

CHAPTER 8

Forgiveness

What I have learned during my period of incarceration is to be very kind and humble. Joseph recognized his brothers, but they didn't recognize him. *"For God caused me to be fruitful in the land of my affliction."* (Genesis 41:52b, NKJV) *"But* *now, do not, therefore, be grieved or angry with yourselves because you sold me here; for God sent me before you to preserve life.* Genesis 45:5, NKJV

Throughout it all He was with me, there were some hardships and let-down moments and a few disappointments. At times anger and resentment were riding my quick temper. Now I'm renewed from it all. I serve a God that is My Father, My Friend; when there is no one to turn to, I know I can count on Him. He died for our sins, I'm so proud to say I truly do love the Lord.

This battle was never mine. I'm forever thankful. David illustrated the importance of trusting in God's control of all things through every affliction. The Lord provided protection and guidance each step of the way. These experiences taught David to trust wholeheartedly in the Lord's control and goodness.

I dedicate this book also to all those who struggle in the war on the battlefield. Just know that God is our strength in our times of weakness.

Taking responsibility and I read this passage over and over again, I just knew it was a great place to start. In David's prayer in Psalm 139:23-24,

NKJV, says, *"Search me, O God, and know my heart; try me, and know my anxieties; and see if there is any wicked way in me, and lead me in the way everlasting."*

We must be willing to face the truth about our inner life and own what's ours. The Lord promises that when we bravely ask for his insight, *"you shall know the truth, and the truth shall make you free."* John 8:32, NKJV

Just like He is at work behind the scenes in my life bringing about exactly what I need and when I need it. He will do the same for you.

CHAPTER 9

We Have an Awesome God

He is all-knowing. Just as God gave resilience to Jeremiah, the prophet would face intense pressure when he delivered unwelcomed messages to Israel, so God promised to make him an "iron pillar a bronze wall." The prophet wouldn't be flattened, dismantled, or overwhelmed. His words would stand strong because of God's presence and rescuing power throughout his life. (Jeremiah 1:18, NKJV)

Jeremiah was falsely accused, arrested, tried, beaten, imprisoned, and tossed into a well; yet he survived. Jeremiah also persisted despite the weight of inner struggles, doubt, and grief that plagued him with constant rejection and the dread of Babylonian invasion added to his mental stress.

God continually helped Jeremiah so that his spirit and testimony weren't shattered. When we feel like giving up on the mission, He has given us not only His strength but the necessary tools to live a faith-filled life. We can remember that Jeremiah's God is our God. He can make us as strong as iron because "His strength is made perfect in our weakness." II Corinthians 12:9, NKJV

"Dear God, please strengthen me to meet the challenges I face today. I ask of these things because I know Your mercy is at work. Lord, I never want to revisit the cycle of hopelessness ever again." I accept my discipline according to Hebrews 12:6, "For whom the Lord loves He chastens, and scourges every son who He

receives." I learned from my mistakes like David in Psalms 139:23-24, "Search me, O God, and know my heart; try me and know my anxieties; and see if there is any wicked way in me, and lead me in the way, everlasting."

I asked the Lord to highlight anything preventing me from moving forward with Him.

Pray without ceasing.
I Thessalonians 5:17, NKJV

CHAPTER 10

My Story

April 3, 1993, I was arrested the following day, I was indicted on charges of 1st-degree felony murder and Strong-Arm Robbery. I went from the humblest guy in school to the cruelest animal in society, with

(25) years to Life minimum mandatory with consecutive (15) years. That was the sentence that was handed down to me.

I was a very bright young man with a positive future ahead. As I was growing up like most guys, I loved sports. I truly was good in all three (3), football, basketball, and baseball. One of my greatest achievements was winning my middle school basketball championship which prepared me for senior high school. Instead, I became a father to my son Dwayne (Buster) and then two (2) years later my daughter was born Chancellor. Now my responsibilities were them. My life revolved around family.

At my first court appearance I was guilty already no trial by jury but, because of news media outlet WSVN Channel 7 publicities. Being a young man that was far from being a murderer.

I was so much into learning and reading so much, until one day I did some research on similar cases pertaining to what I had been charged with. A few famous stars came to mind that were not held accountable opened me up to the unfairness of our justice system. These people had been charged with Hit and Run incidents just to name a few in Miami-Dade

County: Former Cleveland Browns football player, Daunte Stallworth; and famous actress Robin Givens.

They were freed seemingly because they were celebrities and money played a major factor. All that played a part in the deemed justice system to be prejudiced, biased, and very unjust.

The truth of the matter is that I am a supreme being of wisdom, and as well as my character, I've redeemed myself as a man of the Lord.

There was no initial intent of any violence in my life. Being a humble man in life made me wonder. But in the eyes of the judges, and state attorneys I was convicted.

As I sat in the county jail, I had an opportunity to witness the *"O.J. Simpson case."* The key witness on the stand was a crooked cop, the crucial evidence was a pair of gloves. However, in my situation, it was a vehicle; one that I wasn't even the driver nor the perpetrator.

Now I became convinced, perceiving the truth about how people who are living ungodly will deceive you. As I sat down for (817) days before trial I was truly confident that God only held the key to this critical situation that I was in.

As time got closer for me to going to trial, I had an attorney that had been around the court system for decades. Our client-attorney relationship wasn't the best during the court proceedings. He would show up (20) minutes late only entering with a little black pad. All the prosecutors and judges were fully aware of his strategies, antics, and tactics in the courtrooms; which didn't lead to a good outcome.

The fact that the lead prosecutor and lead homicide detectives had planted evidence in a vehicle that I was never in and coached a six (6) year old witness into believing the vehicle he saw was blue, but in his initial statement it was a gold car in color. Only to prove that I was the murderer.

On July 3, 1995, I was sentenced to prison three (3) days before my 25th birthday.

CHAPTER 11

My Calling

Remembering what was instilled in me from the lady of my life my grandmother, Mrs. Elizabeth Green. Here I was a young man thrown in prison where you had to grow up real fast. Being that I was blessed to be raised by my grandmother who taught me the true values of respect, morals, and principles. Most of all how to love God.

My calling was very simple, stay humble, prayerful, and patient and continue to reflect on the goodness of God. As my time began to move in prison, I wasn't the one to just accept defeat. So, I began my appeals process. Although I was still a layman to the law I filed my first 3.850 motion, after being denied my direct appeal. But I knew that the God I serve wouldn't give me more that I couldn't handle.

With God's power, I became very active in Chapel services, staying focused, attaining my G.E.D., and being actively working out. I was focused on getting this conviction overturned because I was innocent in every aspect of the law. Nothing was ever given to me it was earned.

So, I dedicated myself to the Law Library where I would research for days and months at a time. As I continued to file my motions I was constantly getting rejected. I was my own pro-se attorney, I truly had faith in God that I was providing the services that I needed to get the relief sought.

Through it all, I trusted no one but God. As I sit in the Law Library on the computer researching, I heard His voice. *"I am the way, the truth, and the light. No one comes to the Father except through Me." (John 14:6, NKJV) That's the reality, we can live with it forever.*

"Father, thank you for sending your son to provide a way for me to be reconciled to you forever." After praying that prayer back to God, I had to change some things. One, I had to get rid of being angry, which was the easy way out of the path of self-destruction. I learned fast it was a very difficult task to see other inmates and convicts not knowing what to expect. As for me, I learned what to do and how to beat the odds. I had to block the thoughts of my own actions, and take responsibility for creating any of the chaos and suffering I was experiencing now. I came to realize that there is a lot of injustice in this world, and I have been treated unjustly, a miscarriage of justice.

It was so easy to be mad at the world, my change came when I processed it and worked through it to find happiness and fulfillment. At times I felt as if I was on an island by myself surrounded by sharks with nowhere to go.

But I had to get out, start on a book, begin journaling and continue researching my case. Breath... Don't take this at heart I was able to manage my emotions; I even cried to prevent getting angry. It all has kept me focused; being angry doesn't allow you to be happy. The relief I have now has been no one but God, who got me through, What a calling!

Being in the trenches, behind these fences has made me more discipline. It improved my self-development. Being a father that didn't get the opportunity to help raise my children was my most disappointing moment, but I managed. Now I have awesome grandchildren that see a godly man that has made a great impact in their lives.

CHAPTER 12

My Truth

It's not the size of the dog in the fight but the size of the fight in the dog. I was determined not to give up nor give in. I never carried guilt around with me for (30) years I knew God. My faith was that one day someone will recognize my trial and error.

My words and actions were all I had now, it was time to display who I had become; a man of renewal, rebuilt and reinvented. Besides my legal work, my priority was to achieve my goals and dreams. The beginning of this cycle began with self-improvement and finding my inspiration, it held so much emotion and passion.

The emptiness was no longer in my thought process. All I could think of now is how the big things didn't carry any weight nor affect me. The biggest part of my release is that my family doesn't have to worry about coming to see me just to be patted down and sometimes even stripped searched or the K-9 unit outside sniffing the visitors' cars. The suffocating pain was about to end. It was time for me to enter the real world.

My truth is for some change is scary. The man I've become takes a lot of courage, determination, and faith to begin a new path. I've built new friendships by connecting, being committed to trust, and doing the right things. I'm committed to the people who share my beliefs, I do things differently, and I have formed accountability partners on my new journey.

Giving up is not an option, I'm building my new world

filled with peace. In life we all process things differently, for me I have a playbook, it is called the Bible. I executed it, but the plays I was calling weren't working; the moment I laid down all of my burdens, my true blessings came pouring in.

My vision is God has given me this gift to love and share His Word only through Him.

I dedicated this book to every fellow struggler who has had the courage to face the truth about themselves, the humility to abandon their flawed attempts at living, and the willingness to find God's truth and live accordingly to His will.

The man of tomorrow, Apostle Leroy Rogers

www.ingramcontent.com/pod-product-compliance
Lightning Source LLC
Chambersburg PA
CBHW060254150626
46553CB00019BA/2308